Sydney Dobell

Of Parliamentary Reform : A Letter to a Politician

Second Edition

Sydney Dobell

Of Parliamentary Reform : A Letter to a Politician
Second Edition

ISBN/EAN: 9783337134181

Printed in Europe, USA, Canada, Australia, Japan

Cover: Foto ©Suzi / pixelio.de

More available books at **www.hansebooks.com**

OF

PARLIAMENTARY REFORM:

A LETTER TO A POLITICIAN.

BY

SYDNEY DOBELL.

Second Edition.

LONDON:

CHAPMAN AND HALL, 193 PICCADILLY

1866.

LONDON :

RODSON AND SON, GREAT NORTHERN PRINTING WORKS,

PANCRAS ROAD, N. W.

My dear Friend,

You wish me to set forth in a Pamphlet-letter the scheme of enfranchisement to which I alluded in our late conversation on Parliamentary Reform. I think that even your flattering request would not compel me to what must necessarily be a brief and insufficient exposition of that scheme, if I did not care more for its principles—which I shall be glad to see yourself or any other eminent publicist embody more happily—than for the machinery by which I propose to apply them; and if I did not believe that the question of Reform will retain its troublesome Premier-haunting character, till we answer it on principles more organic, expressed in machinery more natural, than those of that provisional and temporary reply which, in 1832, was the best that state exigencies allowed.

But I believe that the principles of the scheme you desire to examine are so conformable to the best order of national development, and so necessary, therefore, to any such change in our institutions as may main-

tain our present place among the progressive nations,
that if, in the following remarks, I find time, and
you patience, for anything like a clear indication of
them, I shall cheerfully forego the attempt to present
you with an elaborate *projet de loi*, and shall not be
seriously disappointed if the claims of more peremp-
tory work, the shortness of my stay in England, and
the limits of any letter that I could conscientiously
inflict, just now, on your busy life, may even oblige
me to offer you my plan without those assistant sta-
tistics and illustrative instances which your wide
knowledge and practised judgment can so readily
supply. I am the less willing to wait for greater
leisure to either of us, because a great national controversy on the subject of Reform seems presaged
pretty plainly for the coming year; and as Parliamentary Reform has come in our day to mean reform
of the popular branch of Parliament, and the patient
is not usually the best judge of his own case, one is
glad to expect that, in this age of journalism, a large
part of the discussion will be outside the House of
Commons. If that expectation be just, the outsiders
should at once begin their irregular portion of the
debate, since it is not the extramural disputations
themselves, but the national mind which they exercise
(and your Giant-politic, having perhaps to clean out
his *rinderpest*, club some Asiatic man-eater, or hold
his bale of cotton for Omphale, is not often quick at
his lessons), that must proximately affect the more
formal controversy indoors. Therefore, and because

one specific advantage of a popular debate should be the outbreak, undeterred by too nice an etiquette, of whatever true thought on the subject in dispute the unceremonial nation can anywhere throw up, I dispense with all modest exordium, and address myself point-blank to the honour you would have me undertake.

If, as I have hinted, Parliament has special difficulties in discussing Parliamentary Reform, arising from the retrospective self-conscious character of the investigation, the non-parliamentary world has also special difficulties, resulting from an opposite cause. If the legislature, with its eyes turned inward, is likely to get no just notion of its own objective personality, we who regard it from without are likely to be too much impressed with the characteristics of its bodily presence. And that bodily presence is, at to-day's point in our history, precisely of the kind on which it is most dangerous to reason, because it is, and has been for more than thirty years (that is to say, during the political life of those who will be most likely to examine it), the questionable shape of a hybrid. A hybrid, as most of us are aware, may be very safe and useful in action, but it is singularly perilous and untractable as an object of scientific inquiry, especially when that inquiry is for the discovery of organic principles. He who looks for horse or for ass in the horse-ass is pretty certain to find it; and even the steadiest judgment will conscientiously see more ass or more horse, according to its natural bias or acquired prejudices.

That wondrous interfusion of differing traits to a new resultant that is neither and both, which we see in the produce of two individuals of the same species, does not exist in the non-propagating hybrid. Its life has no consistent paradigm, and in breeding another creature of the same kind (I hope the illustration may not seem irreverently pastoral), we must decide whether of the two co-operating natures is the more apt to the work for which the hybrid is designed. It may be that by adjusting the relative size and vigour of the parents the quality we seek can be strengthened in the offspring. It may be that new conditions of the work may render it desirable to omit an element formerly useful, and to rear no longer the mule but the horse.

Now, as we all know, the Parliament of England was, up to times quite recent, a means of assisting a governing sovereign, or a governing oligarchy, with what wisdom might be in the nation; and the theory of parliamentary representation, as understood by our earlier jurists, was the rationale of a method for eliminating that wisdom and conveniently presenting it to the ruler. When, however, (as we all also know,) in process of time the sovereign really reigned without governing, that is to say when England, gradually and unconsciously, became the only true and safe republic that ever existed (because, among many "becauses," a republic wherein the highest prize in social rank is impossible to the ambition of any citizen), Parliament virtually assumed to be the *alter ego* of the governing nation, and by parliamentary representation the nation sought to create that other self. The problem was no longer how to extract a certain element from a compound national mass, but how to present, at one time and place, a national epitome, synopsis, and quintessence — in short, the old problem of macrocosm and microcosm.

But as this change in the problem, and in the desideratum it was to yield, was never theoretically stated, and as (faithful to that peculiarity in all our English changes by which we avoid the break of continuity that is mortal to all, except the lowest, living bodies) the modern Parliament and the ancient Parliament differed little in appearance and materials, it was natural that many observers should ignore what had essentially taken place. We had turned the old wisdom-making machine into a kind of demometer, but the two natures in the cross refused to mix; we had configured without metamorphosis, and compounded without transubstantiation. Therefore, while the popular politician honestly discerns in the resulting institution only the modern version of democracy, the conservative eye as honestly perceives only the last form of "Witena Gemot." According to the Witena-gemotic system, the principles on which Parliament should, if needful, be further modified, would seem, at first glance, to be simple and self-evident. Whenever a non-electing class in the nation can demonstrate its equality in whatever qualities are ex-

pressed by "Witena" with any class already possessing the electoral franchise, that non-electing class has
proved its right to share the possession. But, as recent
arguments have indicated, further consideration will
show that this simple formula is not sufficient to the
case, because as, by the hypothesis, an equality with
the enfranchised class possessing the lowest amount
of qualification, entitles any other class to share possession of the franchise, whatever accession of numbers happened to the electing body might happen at
the lowest qualifying degree. And to increase the
number of inferior choosers is, of course, where
majorities are to decide, to deteriorate the chances
of the choice. Therefore, when choosing a "council
of the wise," an equality in choosing power with a
class already privileged to choose, ought not, *per se*,
to entitle a non-choosing class to share the privilege
of choice. But who will ever convince the excluded
class of the justice of their exclusion? Or who can
wonder that the denial of claims which, to the claim-
ants, must appear so logically irresistible, arouse those
heartburnings which, when inflaming great masses of
physical force, end in rebellion and revolution? I
will not pause upon these and other difficulties, in
any theory of parliamentary representation that has
" *wisdom*," in the popular sense, for its final cause,
because (like others whose eye is not specially conservative) my bias sees in our modern Parliament
rather those vital principles by which it may subserve present and future necessities than those by

which, however beautifully and beneficially, it connects the present with the past.

I think that, by the "Reform Act," and by the Parliamentary policy that has succeeded it, we practically gave up the advantages of being governed by others wiser than ourselves (as under our original Parliaments) for certain other advantages supposed to result from *self-government*. But the amount of advantage from self-government—whether individual or national—is (I think the deepest truths of human nature are concerned in this) in proportion to the *selfness* of it. Experience shows (and in this the deepest thinking would forerun experience) that the mistakes and ill-doings of genuine self-government are, in the long-run, more advantageous to the governed, because more conducive to real progress, than the sage anachronisms and out-of-place wisdom of governors whose mental and moral rank is, for other purposes, very far superior to their own. But (and, again, some of the fundamental truths of human nature are concerned) for the errors and wrongs of self-government to be salutary they must be genuine: for the sins we commit under partial compulsion have little, if any, therapeutic effect upon us; and good deeds mechanically done are nearly useless to moral development.

Therefore, by partial self-government we lose, at once, the specific advantages of nationality and bureaucracy—the educational effects of our own right and wrong, and the temporary and superficial

benefits which might accrue from a perfunctory sub-
servience to others. It seems to me therefore that,
in endeavouring to represent the British people in
Parliament, you must, at the stage of national life to
which we are arrived, endeavour towards whatever
may, in the truest, completest, and most living manner, realize self-government;—whatever will, in such
time and place as is consistent with unity of action,
present that British nation which, in a manner
inconsistent with such unity, is spread abroad over
these islands. I say "present" it; for, when theo-
rizing on this subject, we must remember that, in
making Parliament, we are not creating an entirely
vicarious being,—an absolute other self, by whose
substitution we escape all personal activity, and in
whose mere and sufficient proxy we alone have
responsible existence, but a representative agent
whereby we (who occupy such and such territories,
own armies, navies, and a flag, have, at home
and abroad, all kinds of material and immaterial
interests, and will that here, within our own borders,
and elsewhere, the right be done) are *ad extra* to
take not only our place, but our part, in the community of nations, and, *ad intro*, so to act and enact
as shall reach the allegiance, and, in some sort, the
co-operation of the humblest and remotest subject of
this empire.

Now, in representing an individual, whether man
or nation, so that it may virtually be and act, *en
permanence*, in a place where it is not, how must you

represent it? Neither at its best nor its worst; but at the best which it can healthily and continuously maintain. Represent a man in that state wherein he says his prayers, or makes love, or reads poetry, or enjoys fine pictures, or performs an heroic action, and your representation is, for practical purposes, untrue; because no man can healthily maintain himself in that key through all the hours of every day. Represent his lowest possibilities, and you are still more perniciously false. Represent him even at a vulgar mean, below what his qualities can healthily, harmoniously, and continuously reach, and your representation, if he is bound to realise it (and Parliamentary representation is, as we have seen, a representation we are bound to realise), is untrue, and morally deleterious. But represent him at the highest moral, intellectual, spiritual, and physical degree, which, with no more strain than is healthy stimulus, he can consistently and effectively maintain, and your representation, being true to the essential and persistent characteristics of the original, will not only represent him fairly, honestly, and efficiently to others, but, if he is to back it by personal action, will place himself under exactly those fortunate conditions of present exercise which are also the happiest guarantees of beneficial development. If these things be true of just representation when the individual to be represented is a man, they will be found, I think, equally true when the original to be reproduced is that large man a nation. I assume, therefore, that a just national representation is such as represents the nation AT ITS EFFICIENT DURABLE BEST. Granted this kind of representation to be desirable, by what machinery can it be accomplished? Not by such as should merely represent numbers; for numbers, inspired by something that is not due to number, are capable of a higher national life than they could themselves originate. These flesh and bones of the state depend, and seem likely long to depend, for their noblest national character, on the vital life supplied by other functions. Yet numbers must not be unrepresented. You cannot appraise a man's total nature by his bodily weight and forces, but in representing his sum of ability you omit them at your peril. Nor, for similar, but not identical, reasons, is it sufficient to represent property. We want not a democracy—in the modern sense—nor a plutocracy, but a nation: and not only a nation, but, as I have already suggested, a nation at its efficient durable best. Extremes are comparatively easy, and so is vulgar mediocrity; but the healthy best has always been the crucial difficulty of portrait-painter, moralist, and psychologist. And if to create this kind of other-he is difficult when the primary self is an individual man, how much more difficult when the ipsissimus is a nation!

I think there are four obvious methods in which, with more or less success, it might be attempted. One, but the least desirable, would be to represent classes instead of places. You might so represent classes as to create an assembly of intensely typical men, whose correlation of forces might result in such a dynamical mean as should give the strength and direction of thinking and feeling England. The highest philosophy, the merest heroism, the widest knowledge, might leaven the grosser representatives of the (so to speak) popular flesh and blood, to a total that should express the nation at its "efficient durable best." But, apart from the fact of our instinctive English dislike to class representations, this mode would be guilty of a great human waste. We do not want philosophers in the legislature. Their function is to prepare governors and governed for a better than the present best; and their legislation would always, therefore, be that most pathetic kind of failure, the impracticability of beautiful anachronism. Discarding this method, I see three others. You might endeavour so to modify the franchise as to favour a practical union of all the aristocracies—the aristocracy of blood, of talent, of land, of wealth, of science, and of skill — *e. g.* the hereditary "nobility and gentry," the chief thinkers, artists and learners, the exceptional traders, and the skilled artisans—*i. e.* the born "upper classes" of the country, (for the skill of a skilled artisan implies a born aptitude,) against the dead weight of mere numbers and stupid welfare. Or you might, by slightly altering our present modes, make a Parliament of political physicians, able in popular diagnosis, who should do as a legislature what journalism does in another fashion—reproduce, to the best of their power, that which tact, talent, and study teach them to be "Public opinion." Or you might create a self-adjusting electoral machine to do that work in a less conscious and voluntary manner. Of the three former of these methods I say nothing here, except that I would rather not depend on them till the fourth has proved impossible. And of the self-adjusting self-registering machinery for that fourth? Towards some mechanism of this laographical sort I would, with much diffidence, offer the following suggestions:—

The thing of which you would create such another self as you can bring into the palace of Westminster, is not a nomadic or stationary crowd, but that unity a nation. Therefore, in representing its constituent parts, you must represent them in their constituent character. That is to say, in representing the proportionate value of each constituent, you must estimate his part in the size, shape, and weight of that unity, his formative share in the national whole;—i.e. you must represent him not as the man but as the citizen. This large One a nation, is, so to speak, a great Chinese puzzle, made up of different parts, each part differing in size and shape; and in estimating the political value of a man, you require to know not what and how much he is, per se, but what and how much of him goes to the puzzle. You are going to make an enormous national civis, and you must make it by aggregating not men but cives.

You must, therefore, give to each voter who coacts with his fellow-citizens in choosing a representative, such an amount of influence in that choice as shall express his comparative value as a citizen. The special characteristics of a citizen are, I think, those which relate him to his compatriots (including in that term his sovereign and his fellow-citizens) and those which relate him to a certain quantity of the earth and its goods—social relations and, to speak familiarly, "vested interests." (I say "to speak familiarly," because, of course, a man may have an "interest" in the existence of a "relation.") If it is answered that, inasmuch as relations may exist without corresponding virtues, and interests without adequate rights, the representation of relations and interests would not necessarily reach that standard of "efficient durable best" which I have proposed as the test of beneficial representation, I would reply that, in the present state of our laws, and of their administration, the maintenance, without legal punishment, of interests and relations is, taken generally and for practical purposes, sufficient proof and measure of the virtues that should actuate and the rights that should justify them, e. g. that out of a given number of masters and heads of families there will be a large majority in whom those relations indicate the presence of an average amount of the appropriate magisterial and paternal qualities. Therefore, if you represent social relations and vested interests, you are not only representing the outward configuration

of the citizen, his civic size, shape, and weight, and
consequently his constructional value in the national
form, but you also represent (not with the delicacy
of a recording angel, but in as accurate a way as is
usually possible to great human estimates) the virtues
and the rights which are his quota in that total heart,
soul, and conscience, whereby alone the living body-
politic can attain or maintain its "efficient durable
best." Which of the social relations should represent themselves—which of a man's social conditions
as subject, husband, father, master, servant, artisan,
tradesman, ratepayer, landlord, tenant, dealer, capi-
talist, professor, graduate-in-arts, and the like, should
separately represent itself by an electoral vote, and
should therefore add to that sum of votes by which
I would express his comparative importance as a
citizen, is a matter of detail that does not affect principles, and may be left, therefore, to another time
and place. But I would indicate an essential dis-
tinction between relations and interests, which seems
of vital moment, and which is the answer to such
objectors as might demur to the enfranchisement of
interests, on the plea that inasmuch as interests
always involve relations—"property has its duties
as well as its rights" — to enfranchise an interest,
in se, would be to give an undue preponderance to
property. Social relations should be counted in estimating the citizen as a component part of the state,
because (among other reasons) each new relation
which a man protends—each new social office he fills

—binds him to his fellows by a new kind of social obligation. But it is the kind and not the quantity of the obligation that the relation expresses, and, in the majority of cases, it is the kind rather than the quantity that affects his value and character as a citizen. A man with his third wife may be no more husbandly than with his first; and the father of a dozen children and of one may be equally paternal. But when we come to deal with interests, expressing rights, the case is different, because it is not so much the kind, as, so to speak, the quantity of right that expresses a man's shape and weight as a citizen. "The widow's mite" is not to the point, because in the parable it represented not a right but a virtue. If one objects that when legislation takes the widow's mite (which is her "all") it interferes with a larger quantum of right than when it takes the mite of the millionaire, I would answer that, in both cases, it interferes with the right to a mite and no more. If the widow had ten mites, she would have the same right to each of them as to her "one," and she holds her "one" by a right neither larger nor less than that by which she holds each of those decimals. That her one mite when she gives it up to the state may represent as much patriotism as the million pounds of the millionaire is quite true; but in this it is the measure of a virtue and not of a right;—and a measure so difficult of use and gauge as to be unavailable for the rough purposes of human government. Again, her right to a mite

c

may, when the mite is "her all," involve other rights, as *e. g.* the right to life. But this involution is not in virtue of her interest in a mite but her interest in her "all," which is in an entirely other category, and would be dealt with on other legislative principles than those of ordinary fiscal legislation. The *allness* of the mite represents its size and shape in the economy of the owner, the *miteness* of it represents, so far as it can be represented by property, the owner's bodily size and shape in the economy of the nation. I say "bodily" size and shape, for every man not a felon or (in the absolute sense) a pauper, has, viewed as a subject for legislation, a dual existence—he exists *per se*, and by the proxy of his goods. Legislation cannot move without impinging on goods; but as it never affects them as possessions of tenants in common, or as a copartnery of equal shares, the size of that second existence is a quantity differing in every citizen. While that impersonal-looking statute that impartially levies so much in the hypothetical pound practically means that, though I and my neighbour look so much alike, I am to pay a trifle and he is to bleed thousands a year, it is as evident that my neighbour's real personality is, as regards this law, greater than mine, as if he had personally stretched out before the tax-gatherer an anaconda length of living substance to visible infliction. While, therefore, the real self of one man so differs from that of another, self-government surely requires a representative expression of that

difference; whether that difference consist in the
differing number of functions whereby a man assists
in composing that total citizen the state, or in the
differing size of his share in that great partnership,
whereby (to use an analogue not quite perfect) this
political corporation holds its lands and goods. And
those who propose to find that expression in a plu-
rality of votes, are only adopting, for parliamentary
elections, a machinery which, in regard to the smaller
elections for parochial parliaments, has already the
assent of the country. They may fairly suggest
also that, perhaps, the idea of plural voting has been
recognised in English political life from time im-
memorial, and might inquire whether the facts that
some districts return one and some two members to
Parliament—*i. e.* that each elector in the one has
double the choosing power of his compatriot in the
other—and that the same elector may have a vote
for more than one locality—*i. e.* that as concerns the
total result of a general election his choosing power
may be multiplied to any extent of which locomotion
will allow—are not of that germinal kind that con-
tains a developable principle, and do not so far
nullify the entire electoral equality that has been
claimed for our system as to throw doubt on the
fundamental character of it? However this may be,
I am aware of the objections which will spring to
the imagination of many politicians, when I propose
that the vote of every British subject, unconvicted of
crime, shall be taken at the elections of members to

serve in Parliament, but shall be reckoned (according to some scale to be fixed after due parliamentary inquiry) at a value commensurate with the number of his social relations and the extent of his rights of property:—counting one for the man, if any such exist, who is only a subject, and so on, upwards, for every other.

That is to say, I would propose that the total of votes (by minorities and majorities) at a general election should represent the total of civic functions that make up that vast civis the nation, and the total of lands and goods which he rightfully possesses; and that the number of these votes given by any one civiculus (so to speak) should indicate the value of him and his in the composition of those national wholes. Believing that a plan of this kind is likely to secure the end I have ventured to propose as the object of all beneficial representation—the representation of the thing represented "at its efficient durable best"—I would beg the further patience of yourself and your friends while I point out some other advantages which seem to inhere in such a system.

1. To ascertain the electoral qualifications of an elector would require no new or inquisitorial machinery. As I propose to enfranchise not moral or intellectual qualities, but the civic functions which, on the average (and an average quite as high as that of the political ability indicated by tenancy of a 10*l.* or a 6*l.* house), are their social signs, and not abstract rights, but those possessions which, when unques-

tioned by the law, are their sufficiently accurate evidence, the new franchise would have to take cognisance of nothing that was not already recognised and identified by title-deeds, diplomas, tax-receipts, licenses, parish-registers, apprenticeship-indentures, and the like unmistakable testimony. It is not amenable, therefore, to the strong arguments that have been urged against a metaphysical franchise.

2. As entirely comprehensive and self-adjusting, it would be likely to save us from those eras of organic change which, viewed from within or without, have hitherto been the great perils of constitutional peoples. Descending at once to the lowest possible, and making the *personnel* of the constitution commensurate with the nation, you rest it, so to speak, on that immoveable basis of the earth whereon terrestrial things can alone be permanent, instead of poising it, as at present, on a seething mass of incongruous life,—like those carved Italian pulpits whose supports are running beasts and fighting men. At the same time, by such a system, the passage of the " lowest" classes in the State to great political power would happen, without convulsion or organic strain, in proportion as they added to their numerical force those civic functions which raise them in the scale of virtual citizenship,—that is to say, in proportion as they became part of the nation's " efficient durable best."

3. It would save us from universal suffrage, popularly so called. To resist that most mortal of all enemies to human progress without denying any

claims that can, by proving themselves consistent
with that progress, show presumptive (or by proving
themselves advantageous to it, show conclusive) proofs
that they are rights, is surely among the first present
duties of British statesmanship. By enfranchising
every non-criminal British subject, and ending that
indefinite consciousness of half - understood wrong
which must exist in every man whose political existence is denied (however just to eyes that do not see
from his standpoint such a denial may be), you
relieve the State for ever from a great chronic danger
which any lassitude or incompetence in those who,
from time to time, adjust the political safety-valves,
may convert into the most active maleficent force.
" Universal suffrage"—the plan, *i. e.* of ringing up
the servants to settle your vexed questions of philosophy, art, and morals—has too little attraction for
the English order of mind to be ever an indigenous
danger; but as it is in full force in nations with
whom every day is bringing us into more sympathetic
union, we are likely, without preventive care, to
receive, by infection, a disease not congenital to
British common sense. For that preventive care no
mere theoretical demonstration will suffice. To convince the reason that "universal suffrage" is unrea-
sonable will be useless, so far as the excluded classes
are concerned, while feeling answers that its denial
involves the refusal of a right, and its establishment
the removal of a wrong. To show that what is called
"universal suffrage" is not "universal" at all (since

the suffrage of the beaten minority is not represented
in the result), but really means absolute choice by
whatever party happens to be the most numerous;
that, in the present (and every other immature) state
of the world, that condition of mind which chooses ill,
under difficulties, is more common than that which
chooses well; that therefore, when numbers choose,
their choice (deducting a small percentage for exceptional cases) will be erroneous; that the knowledge
of this will deter the best men from offering themselves to electors who are known, à priori, to prefer
the inferior, and that from an assembly of "the inferior" the various interplay of moral attraction and
repulsion would soon eliminate the small percentage
of better whom accident might have intruded on it;
that an assembly thus finally representing only the
inferior elements of a nation, so far from realising
that "efficient durable best" which is the necessary
condition of beneficial representation, because the
only condition of national life which is truly favourable to individual and collective progress, must exercise the national being precisely in that manner
whereby men and nations deteriorate, and by degrad-
ing its own individuality, and withdrawing it more
and more from its just partnership in the community
of peoples, eventually make its political existence a
menace to the civilised world; to show all this, and
conclude that such an electoral system is one of the
most preposterous mistakes and deceptions by which
the half-thinking of sentimental or passionate theorists,

and the policy or profligacy of astute or desperate adventurers, ever caught the multitudes whose perilous intelligence, like the eye with which the salmon sees the hook-bearing sham, is enough for temptation, but insufficient for judgment, will avail nothing to convince these very multitudes, while the grievance of an exclusion, which no reasoning can disprove, is agitating, by the ignominy of odious comparison, those passions which are the common life of all men. Nor will it avail much more to point across the Atlantic, where, with a thousand exceptional conditions to favour the experiment, the system, even thus early in the national history, has notoriously shut out the best minds of America from politics, and set nearly every tuning-fork of public opinion to the lower key-notes of the country: nor across the Channel, where, with whatever apparent temporary success, the worst evils of the machine are corrected by Imperial interference, and to show that this mode of amendment is as faulty in principle as we know it to be demoralising in practice. Setting aside such an exceptional event as that conflux of causes whereby the present Emperor reigns, it may safely be laid down that if, in the countries of universal suffrage, the heads of the State are not such men as universal suffrage would naturally select, they have, by their own hypothesis, no right to govern; and that if, on the other hand, they are truly the exponents of that suffrage, their interference in the further action of the electoral machine merely completes the vicious circle of that pernicious consistency whereby the excelsior arc of the national whole is perpetually wheeling under, the upward shoots of popular life continually contorted towards the ground, the mounting virtues and abilities which are the natural captains of progress incessantly reduced to the ranks, and the nation which, by encouraging what is best, highest, and most beautiful within it, and setting itself to those, should be a vast school of human and national advancement, converted, by deliberately making a goal of zero, a lesson of ignorance, and a standard of " ipsissimum vulgus," into an enormous engine of personal, social, and political retrogression.

These *argumenta ad homines* are useless, because they appeal to precisely that knowledge of human character, and to that political wisdom, which the classes addressed are certain not to possess. To the ploughman, the difference in statesmanship between Lord Palmerston and Mr. Stanton is inappreciable; but he perceives quite well, if he had no vote for the one, that any ploughman in America might, so far as qualification goes, have voted for the other.

By representing every man's comparative weight in the state, instead of enfranchising a mere unit of number, I believe that you would satisfy whatever may be just in the claims of numbers as numbers, while you counteract the possibility of a numerical despotism; and you, therefore, attain the advantages of universal suffrage without those evils by which it has been the bane of politics, and which must rank it as an electoral system—whether such system be considered as an engine of present welfare or as a progress-machine—among the least rational adaptations of means to ends, by which those semi-passions that so often pass for reason have humoured the desires, apologised for the foregone conclusions, and hocussed the fumbling conscience of mankind.

4. It is favourable to hereditary monarchy. By the polarity of things, democracy—when it means the rule of the multitude—must always be liable to Cæsarism, and that Cæsarism may virtually include the four-year king, called president, late American events have suggested. I need not here go into the argument by which it would be easy to prove that *elective* monarchy—called by whatever name—is as incompatible with the political machinery of a true republic as it is injurious to the moral, spiritual, and artistic life of the people who create it; and that the only royalty that consists with the full necessities of constitutional freedom is a function of the body-politic too exquisitely fine to be made and remade periodically by the rude hands of voting millions. That positive of so many negations, that aureole of reflex rays and refracted colours, that cerebral plexus of converging and reverting nerves and forces, is impossible to the turbulence of popular change; only in the unshaken quiet of absolute security can the undisturbed elements take the fortunate concurrence. But though the argument for hereditary monarchy is so well understood in England that I may assume

its conclusions for granted, it may be well to point out that hereditary monarchy, to be a political success, must find among the people consistent habits of thought and congruous social institutions. If not, the gilded car of royalty ballooning in mid-air above the levels of " Liberté, Egalité," will become an idol or a popinjay ; or the king, standing in midst of those levels, will soon, since a king's stature is not necessarily greater than a subject's, be run down by the contempt of multitudinous familiarity. In other words, royalty in the one case, too far removed from the common people to be the object of useful criticism, and surrounding itself—since kings are men, and have men's necessities of love and friendship—with a self-created cabal of favourites, would become a peril to liberty, or an exasperating mark for popular passions : in the other case, the exigencies of daily life would so vulgarise the king and his function, that the idea of the function would be lost in that of the man—a loss mortal to hereditary rule unless in those exceptional kingdoms founded, so to speak, by demigods, whose superhuman longevity is represented rather than succeeded by their heirs. The present French empire is an instance of this rare kind, and should never be counted among elective monarchies. You remember the guardsman's answer to the news that the first Napoleon was dead, —"Lui mort ! vous le connaissez bien !" That touching answer, unsurpassed in history, was really the answer of France. It was as vicegerent of this unconquerable immortality that Louis Napoleon came to power, and though a thousand evidences of statesmanship have since confirmed his title to his uncle's throne, the patent by which he took it was signed and dated in St. Helena.

But in ordinary kingdoms, it is the monarchy rather than the monarch that is, and ought to be perennial; and that part of the popular imagination which conceives general notions has so little native force, that it requires to be protected from the competition of those keen personal images which, though, as our happy experience shows, they may occasionally dignify the ideas they represent, may also, and (since hereditary succession cannot guarantee personal character) more often, degrade or supersede them. I believe that some such electoral system as that which I have ventured to propose would favour among the people those habits of thought and that social attitude which would furnish a new safeguard to the great monarchical abstraction. By associating with the popular notion of progress the notion of constitutional permanence, and with the popular idea (because with the popular practice) of liberty and civic fraternity the idea of personal and political inequality, and by creating among citizens the recognition and the exercise of a graduated order of power, I think it would prove not only the best expositor of popular rights, but would tend also to conserve that hereditary royalty without which (or its yet unknown substitute) no true republic can long exist.

5. It is at once Protestant and Catholic, and a guarantee, therefore, against the extension of Roman Catholic influence. Protestantism, of all varieties, must always rely upon the thinking and half-thinking classes; while, if the papacy is to exist, its future strength must be the millions. It must always rule through the very high or the very low. It is too well read to believe immediately that new facts are endurable; but when changes evidently irresistible show that power is never more to be won from the fears and hopes of a king, it will try the other pole of the same magnet and find it in the depths of the people. Hitherto its political strategy has been the mastery of an exceptional few of peculiar position, education, and resulting character, whose royal desire for the privilege of sinning safely, and known ability to pay for it royally, made them the special customers of "St. Peter." Henceforth the one prince is carved into ten or twenty million; and since, in the nature of things, a like entourage of cardinals, bishops, confessors, or what not, can no longer be spent in the reduction of each unit in this multitude, the deficiency in available force will suggest a change in the character of the campaign. Twenty cacciatori may hardly manage a tiger, but one may suffice for a whole parish of sparrows. By a change in the nature, not of the sportsman but of the game, and a slight corresponding modification in the weapons, the disposable power of the Roman hierarchy may still do immense execution. Prey, adequately weak

however, can usually be found only among the least
intelligent of mankind; but as in the countries of
universal suffrage, these classes must, for the next half-
century, have a vast majority, it is exactly they who
will be the possessors of sovereign power. The *parti
prêtre* will soon perceive that in those countries universal suffrage means the despotism of the masses,
and that the despotism of the masses means the
despotism of those by whom the masses are swayed;
that is to say, that the problem of obtaining political
influence there, is the problem of obtaining personal
and individual influence over the most ignorant and
least able men and women in them. That personal
and individual influence, entirely independent of
reason or virtue, the wise machinery of the Romish
Church precisely enables it to acquire, and its admi-
rable adaptivity will soon—unless, in fulfilment of
the classic line, it has already entered the dementian
phase of a damnatory fiat—devise some such further
instruments of popularity as may enable it for a time
to besiege its enemies with the very troops they had
mustered for its destruction. It may be said that
these considerations apply to the continents of Europe
and America, but are foreign to British interests.
Without pointing to Ireland as a fulcrum for any
papal Archimedes who may wish to try his hand at
"the world," I would suggest that at the present era
it may be wise to foreclose the possibilities of any
class by which Romanism may exercise pressure upon
Parliament. The Church of England will probably

exist as a personality long after, by that irresistible endosmosis and exosmosis whereby her ablest thinkers are already unintentionally assimilating her to the heterodoxy of the external world, her present creed has passed insensibly into the next forward stage of spiritual transformation. When Parliament, in due season, has to formularize that change, it will be of the gravest importance that its action be purely expository, and that no temporary exertions of a party, to whichever meeting extreme of the Roman circle that party may belong, should put an institution so powerful for good or evil, and so certain— from the stability of its wealth, honours, and influence —to rouse all sacred and mundane ambitions, out of harmony with "the efficient durable best" of the nation to which it belongs.

6. It would give a higher sanction to the action of Government on minorities.

When we say that a nation electing its representatives by this or that kind of franchise would be self-governed, we mean, of course, that the dominating party or parties in it would be self-governed. However much you may attempt to "represent minorities," there must always be a residue of unrepresented nonconformity, who must submit to a government in which they had no direct share. Towards such minorities, whether large or small, the party or union of parties, which is politically, for the time being, the nation, acts as man to man. It may, therefore, be of the greatest importance that the title of the one to temporary empire should be such as commands the conscience of the other. In quiet times the more conventional and superficial considerations for which the loser submits to the winner (as, for instance, the compact to abide by the results of an appeal to numbers, which is implied by electoral coaction) are sufficient to insure the good-humour of the game; but in great crises it may be of vital consequence that the few thinkers who, in all parties, control the many workers, should be able to recognize more radical claims to respect. Now, in actions between individual men, an agent's highest claim to act is, that he acts in his moral right. The highest presumptive evidence that he is in his moral right is, therefore (short of absolute demonstration), the best available evidence of his title to act. That the proof of his title to act would not necessarily be proof of his title to act unopposed, may be very true; but if it immensely increases the gravamen and responsibilities of opposition, its political value is nearly as great. Now a nation acting by an organism that represents its efficient durable best, offers the highest presumptive evidence that it acts in its moral right; and comes therefore to a dissident minority, with the highest available title to empire. If you were merely a politician, in the vulgar sense of the word, I should not trouble you with the theorem of which this proposition is corollary; but, knowing that you and I are seldom satisfied with any branch of arts or science unless we can, more or less clearly, see back to its bifurcation with the universal Igdrasil, I would merely beg you to remember, while examining it, the disadvantages under which, in this letter, so synoptical an argument must be stated.

I say not only "in a letter," but "in this letter," because I know you wish to show it to many of your friends, and I must therefore avoid the technique of philosophy.

Man being imperfect and perfectible, and moral philosophy, therefore, a department of embryology, I would say that the being and doing of a perfect human creature is the standard of absolute human good.* But as we are all at present imperfect, how is this standard to be utilised?

The difference between the perfect and the imperfect is not a difference of kind but of development. Therefore the good of any perfectible imperfect human creature,—whether man or nation,—is (not perfunctory imitation of a perfect specimen, but) such being and doing as develop it towards perfection. That is to say, that a perfectible's good cannot be the subject of exact definition, *extra se*, inasmuch as it differs not only for each perfectible but for each phase of the same perfectible: in other words, that it comes not under the science of morals, as usually understood, but under the science (and art) of education, properly so called. Now the science of edu-

---

* I must ask you to wait a little longer for that still unfinished book, so often promised to your friendly questions, in which I have endeavoured to apply this standard to the cosmos of human affairs.

cation should show us that every perfectible being has an autonomy according to which its development proceeds; but that the relation of any stage of progress to final perfection is to be judged not by phenomenal likeness (since this does not always increase in the ratio of succession), but by its place in the autonomical order. The case being so, there must be great difficulty in defining for any being the earliest limit of passive good; but we may safely say of any change,—e. g. of any activity,—that if in the perfectional order of development, it is good. (Of course there may be cases, as of over-development or unhealthy development, or of moral evil reacting in greater good, where retrogression may be essential progress, but these are abnormal.)

Now though man is a complex unity of many comparatively simple beings, each having its autonomy, natural history, and personal welfare, but each and all subserving the autonomy of the whole, and though there are some peculiarities which still further complicate the problem of man,—for instance, that his progress in the perfecting order not only requires (as in the embryology of all complex creatures) changes in collocation and proportion of parts, but some curious illustrations of (so to speak) isomerism and isomorphism, as well as (perhaps) certain excretory or exfoliatory processes, we may still apply to him the foregoing formula of good. For though that activity of the whole in the perfectional order of development, which is its "law" of good, may not

always consist with the individual welfare of all the
parts (that is to say, may interfere with perfectionating them as wholes, in order to perfectionate them
as parts), and though, at the same time, a certain conformity to the sanitary conditions of these "parts," as
individuals, is necessary to the health of the whole
(and health is a *sine quâ non* of moral development),
this correlation of forces is a problem to be worked
out for every new case, and does not interfere with
the general principle; inasmuch as whatever may,
ipso casu, be that co-estate and co-activity of parts
which can be proved to advance the whole in
the perfectional order, conforms to the "law" of
good.

But man is not an unreasoning creature, unconsciously developing and ignorantly realising that
"relative good" by which he will attain perfection.
He is a *mens sibi conscia recti*,—a self-conscious mind,
not only doing and being good, but having ideas of
it and of himself in relation to it. These ideas shape
his moral right. The mental function concerned with
them seems to be that plexus of abilities commonly
called "conscience." This plexus seems to have two
signal characteristics: the aptitude to receive moral
ideas *ab extra*, whether as abstractions or as images;
and the power (usually accompanying special aptitudes) to sccern a mirage of them, when deprived of
the natural object. Now education, anthropology, or
howsoever you would name that branch of embryology, the science of developing-man, shows that in

the favourable diagnosis and prognosis of his advance in the perfectional order, and of the existence of those internal relations between conscience and the rest of him which constitute morality, there are some cardinal signs. Among these are: the content by the conscience of the highest notions of human perfection which it can, at the given time, honestly hold : the best conformity thereto which the remainder of his abilities can honestly, consistently, and healthily maintain. Turning from the science to the art of education, we may say, therefore, that these are the most favouring conditions of his good. Deducting from these conditions what is external to himself, this is to say, in other words, that a man is most likely to be relatively good and morally right when his powers and qualities are co-existing at their efficient durable best, and that to establish the fact of that coexistence is to establish the highest probability of that good and right. Therefore, granting that what is true for that human multiplicity in unity, the individual man, is true for that human multiplicity in unity, the individual nation, a people represented at its efficient durable best, and acting by that representation, offers to all challengers, and among others to any dissident minority that for the time may separate itself from the national whole, the highest attainable guarantee that it acts in its moral right, and, therefore, the most authoritative human claim to the respect of moral beings.

7. It offers the best securities to liberty.

What is true liberty?

We have seen that the being and doing of a perfect human being, whether man or nation, furnish the standard of absolute human good; and that relative human good is such being and doing as are, for the given creature, in the order of progress towards perfection. True liberty is the freedom for such being and doing. Now if, as we may safely take for granted, in a society of imperfect, perfectible beings, the relation of no two beings to perfection is exactly the same, the good of each must differ from that of his neighbour, and his liberty must therefore differ also. There may be those whose liberty is a freedom nearly absolute, and there may be those, on the other hand, whose truest liberty is little more than the freedom of willing not to be free. But if a million citizens have a million differing liberties, how are they to be harmonized? Organize the million, and apply to that complex human unit the organized million what you have found to be valid for that complex human unit the individual man. The million-fold unit may exact from the units which compose it what each of these units may exact from its constituents—just so much and no more subordination of the autonomy of each part as is necessary for the autonomy of the whole; i. e. just so much modification of its perfectionating order as a whole as may be necessary to "perfectionate" it as a part; i. e. so much personal sacrifice in each of the million as may put the million-fold person in the order of its perfection, and may realize for it, therefore, the conditions of its moral good. Now we have found—I need not again go through the progress of finding—that any human being, man or nation, gives the highest presumptive evidence that he is in his perfectional order when he shows that he is and does at his efficient durable best. Therefore, a nation represented at its efficient durable best offers the highest proof that human fallibility permits of its right to control the personal liberty of every citizen who is a constituent of that representation. On such citizens as, not being represented, form part of a minority in such a state, I have already shown that the dominant majority have the highest attainable claims to respect. I think, therefore, I may fairly claim that, whether as regards the ruling majority or the dissentient minority, a nation represented at its efficient durable best offers the highest guarantees for true constitutional liberty. Indeed may it not almost be said that a just realization of true liberty —*i. e.* of such relative liberty as is true to a given point in human progress — is only probable to a nation so organized: because no other nation is likely, as a nation, to have such ideas of right and wrong as are exactly congruous with its place in human history, or, dealing with events as they arise, could so completely concrete *ad hos* and upon them, so to speak, the unwritten law existing at the time and place in the given phase of the national conscience?

I believe that, in our own day, for example, we

hardly guess how much such a people might safely simplify legislation, or how modest and sparse might be that well-placed and little-seen police of law, enforcing merely the primary and necessary conditions of all progress, by whose agency the great human concourse of moral liberties might march at all paces, in all measures, in how many aberrations, and to what discordant tunes, along the mighty highway of political freedom.

8. By representing property—*i. e.* by establishing a ratio between a man's legislative power and the extent of his liability to legislation—you subserve the principle of self-government (for self-government cannot fully exist if the quantum of my power to legislate bears no proportion to the area I offer to legislative impact) while by ballasting the restlessness of discontent with the salutary inertia of those who are satisfied, and exposing the cheap courage which risks the goods of others to the cautious censorship of self-interest, you make change sufficiently laborious to guarantee the safety of progress. And by thus giving a legal existence to the just influence of property, you starve out those illegal forms of political corruption by which at present it so balefully asserts itself, and which show such tenacity of injurious life because they have root in one of those half-rights which no law dares authorize, but which no large justice can absolutely condemn. At the same time, by representing numbers, intelligence, and character, you insure us against " Plutocracy "

—which, as has been well said, is of all "cracies" the most intolerable to a noble nation,—and provide us with a political body, which, while sufficiently coarse to incorporate, in good healthy heavy workable bulk, the subtle forces of the national soul, and preserve us from the dangers of "ideal" politics, shall be true to those organic principles whereby, in all living things whose arena is the earth (the finer in the fine permeating the less fine that enters the gross, and pushing, by those sheaths, into the dense), the deadest obstruction of matter is informed with the controlling immateriality of life, and finally, in our dull mortal fashion, opened to the safe access even of "dominating ideas."

9. By representing "character" and "intelligence," you satisfy the cry for enfranchising intelligence and character; but by increasing the electoral value of each man in proportion as he is mental, moral, and serviceable, instead of endeavouring to give form and political activity to such abstractions as "intelligence," "virtue," or any other concept, you avoid the danger of creating monsters (for every human function or attribute dissected out from the rest, and invested with separate and active existence is monstrous) which must sooner or later evince their abnormity—as in historical precedents they have evinced it—by preying on the wholesome complexities of natural life.

10. By any system that, combining the advantages without the dangers of democracy, oligarchy,

and monarchy, shall realise the efficient durable best
of the British race inhabiting these islands, we shall
maintain that exemplary position by which it seems
to be the vocation of that race to assist the education
of mankind. Such an incarnation of an autonomy as,
if not the final perfection of the creature, shall be
a natural phase of the ordered change that culmi-
nates in perfection, should be the object of every one
who, in any department of constructive art, en-
deavours to follow the Divine process of creation.
A nation realising its "efficient durable best" would
certainly be such an incarnation; and whatever
nation first achieved it would have the right, *de
facto*, to expect a great part in the world, and a
great formative influence on all future political
changes. But if that nation were British, the event
would be additionally significant, because precisely
one of those complementary facts that—like a half-
discovered planet, guaranteed, while yet invisible, by
the necessities of an extant solar system—complete
the consistency of things already established. The
more intimately we know the other tribes of civilised
men, the more we must perceive that, though they
are likely to excel us in particular functions of human genius, the special conditions of our origin and
growth have given the body corporate of the British
people that truth to all manhood, that generic hu-
manity of intense anthropomorphism (as opposed to
the disembodied notions of speculators, or the cha-
racterless indifferentism of weak races), which fit it

E

not only to expound the total progress of Europe,
but to be the pivot-man, time-keeper, pitch-pipe,
root-stem, or by whatever other metaphor from the
arts you may express a living and dominating fact
to which none of them have a precise analogue, of
that slow universal transfiguration which is working
out the destiny of man. By a self-sustaining, self-
adapting, self-registering political organisation, which
shall amply, freely, and accurately give effect to
our compound nationality, we shall best fulfil this
splendid office, and best, therefore, insure that permanence therein whereby the system of nature re-
wards all special aptitudes. Qualifying ourselves for
this proud position towards the world at large, by
measures primarily taken with no ambition to that
end, but honestly chosen for their supposed subser-
vience to our most direct and personal duties, who
knows that we may not unconsciously attain to the
mysterious splendour of something even yet more
sacred? The day may be far distant, and its supreme
glory may not be for these latitudes, when a nation
of perfect men and women, perfectly expressing itself, may be, so to speak, the national Λογος of social
and political truth; but — as the clean hands and
pure heart, even of men still imperfect, have before
now dispensed the Divine Spirit—who shall say how
soon, or how often, in the intervening future, a noble
and Christian people, true, within and without, to
its "efficient durable best," might utter by its legislation, and exemplify by its practice, a *vox populi*

as yet unknown in the modern world—a voice that should prove the hackneyed adage to have been like many another bad proverb, the prophecy of those who, out of due time, perceived as accomplished fact the necessary possible?

Finishing the last sentence, I seem to hear the deafening rataplan of that great drum whereby, in the plaza or piazza of a Spanish or Italian fair, or at some market-day street-corner of Provence or Languedoc, the conjuror and "medicine-man" of Southern Europe summons the crowd to his pharmaceutical wares. With what complacent head-shakes of superior knowledge he lifts the arm of the dislocated skeleton, fits ball to socket, and pumps it into representative action! How paternally his smiling care picks out the baby's skull from the travelling arcanum, spikes it tenderly on the little back-bone, and nurses the "far too naked" mannikin! In how cheerful a confidence he afterwards descants on his panacea, and compels you to the pilulæ juventutis or elixir immortalitatis!

This spontaneous association of ideas is, I confess, hardly flattering; but its spontaneity suggests that it is not wholly unjust. I cannot, it is true, compete with the conjuror in anatomy, philanthropy, or eloquence; but my alkahest may, perhaps, seem warranted to cure all diseases, and inaugurate Utopia and Atlantis. While disclaiming every disposition towards such a warranty, however, I must admit that, in one respect, the conjuror's medical science and mine may not be at all dissimilar. His bread-pills will, I believe, have little violent effect on the present condition of the patient; but if they save him from drugs of positive and mortal activity, they may be the second causes of welfare to himself and benefit to his friends through whatever earthly years of healthy life and vital progress may seem good to the God by whom men and nations live.

At any rate, whatever you think of the nostrum,

Believe me, yours affectionately

SYDNEY DOBELL.

Noke Place, near Gloucester.

LONDON :
ROBSON AND SON, GREAT NORTHERN PRINTING WORKS,
PANCRAS ROAD, N.W.